Fighting Fear With Your Faith

Dr. Lonnie W. Brown

Dr. Lonnie W. Brown
Kingdom of Heaven Ministries
G-3196 W. Pasadena Avenue
Flint, Michigan 48504
(810) 732-5880
ISBN 13: 978-0-9823972-7-5
ISBN 10: 0-9823972-7-5

Table of Contents

Introduction

There is no greater force for the believer than the force of faith that God has deposited inside of His Word. This force can only be experienced as anointed vessels preach the **Word of God,** which informs, enlightens, and reveals **God's** plan for Kingdom expansion and world Dominion. The only other force that is equal in strength for the believer is the force of righteousness. What is the force of righteousness?

God had some things in His heart concerning us. **He** said them out of **His** mouth and they became a reality in **His** world. When we say out of our mouths and believe in our hearts what **God** said concerning us, those things become a reality in our world. Romans 1:16-17 says:

Rom 1:16 ¶ For I am not ashamed of the gospel of Christ: for it is the power of God unto salvation to every one that believeth; to the Jew first, and also to the Greek.

Rom 1:17 For therein is the righteousness of God revealed from faith

to faith: as it is written, The just shall live
by faith.

Inside of the principle of salvation is an in-
depth and detailed understanding of the force
of righteousness. This powerful force is on tap
and available for every believer. When this
force is activated it wields the power of the
Word of God in the mouth of the believer.
This power causes the believer to be invincible
against any force on earth or from the pit of
hell, whose intent is to stop the believer from
realizing his or her specific or collective
purpose in the earth.

The only force that seems to be capable of
counteracting or nullifying these two twin
powers is the force of fear. As believers we
must learn to stand strong against the
tormenting forces and tides of fear with the
Force of Righteousness and the **Word of
Faith** in our mouths. Submit yourself therefore
to God; resist the devil and he will flee from
you. As we submit to the **Force of
Righteousness** and the **Word of Faith** we
will watch fear, prompted by the devil, literally
flee from us.

Remember, the word of God says faith

comes by hearing.

Rom 10:17 _So then faith cometh by hearing, and hearing by the word of God._

The only way we will be able to overcome the onslaught of fear attacking our righteousness is to position ourselves to be constantly under the influence of the Word of God. We must deny worldly information from penetrating our mind, will and emotions. A strict diet of consistently hearing God's word is the only remedy.

Recently, I challenged the congregation that I pastor to take 30 minutes a day to digest the truths ministered from the pulpit. I shared with them that constantly listening to the network news will cause their confidence to be in what they are hearing and not in God's word.

So, how can we overcome the control of fear? Someone once said that there is nothing to fear but fear itself. This seems to be a trite statement in the face of ominous information, circumstances, situations and conditions. What does it really mean, that there is nothing to fear but fear itself? I read an acrostic definition of fear many years ago. It reads as follows:

Fear is:

F = **F**alse
E = **E**vidence
A = **A**ppearing to be
R = **R**eal

I believe with all of my heart that the person who wrote this definition was very sincere. I fully understand that in light of the truth coming from the Word of God, what appears to be true may not be true after all. However, this definition may some how suggest that while it is false it has a nonexistent place in the natural realm. That is to say, it stands without natural, factual support.

I have discovered that there are some things that are factually present in our lives that need a tactical understanding of how they must be dealt with and removed. We must remove the control that they have over us by removing the fear.

With that thought in mind, I believe the Holy Spirit has impressed upon me a different slant on that definition.

Fear is:

F = **F**actual
E = **E**vidence
A = **A**ttacking your
R = **R**ighteousness

> ***Fear*** *is faith threatening opposition determined to undermine your hope, causing you to surrender and abdicate your freedom by aborting the development and fulfillment of vision.*

3 Key elements:

- **Apprehension:** uneasiness, nervousness and hesitancy
- **Anxiety:** restless, overly concerned, and worried
- **Alarm:** troubled, upset, and distressed

I will address this definition in great detail later. I believe there are some tangible things in our environment that can create a level of apprehension that prompts uneasiness, nervousness, or hesitancy about moving forward. Therefore, I submit to you that these things must addressed, dismantled and stripped of their authoritative presence in our lives.

We must not succumb to the threats they offer us, however factual they are. They must be stripped of their control over us. We can no longer allow them to rule, direct and manage our lives.

In order to defeat a force as strong as this we will need a force greater than it. I would like to share with you eight simple keys that can assist you in taking fear out. As you internalize and meditate upon these keys, you will see that facing your fears will be without threat, and taking them out will be a pleasure. In order for us to understand how to take control over fear, there are eight things that we will need to consider.

I would like to introduce you to some marvelous tools that will cause you, the believer, to stand with the freedom to face your fears and defeat every one of them. **First,** understand the leading causes of heart failure. **Second,** understand the nature of terror. **Third,** arm yourself with a weapon against terror. **Fourth,** know that you are secure from terror. **Fifth,** know how to remove the apprehension. **Sixth,** know the secret of arresting anxiety. **Seventh,** know how to turn off the alarm. **Finally,** know the remedy for fear. Now, let's settle back, relax, and examine the strategies of *Fighting Fear With Your Faith*.

CHAPTER ONE

WHAT IS THE LEADING CAUSE OF HEART FAILURE?
Luke 21:25-26
Leviticus 26:36-39

Luke 21:25 And there shall be signs in the sun, and in the moon, and in the stars;

and upon the earth distress of nations, with perplexity; the sea and the waves roaring;

Luke 21:26 Men's hearts failing them for fear, and for looking after those things which are coming on the earth: for the powers of heaven shall be shaken.

These verses give us keen insight into the cause of heart failure. In verse 25 we see how perplexity and danger can capture our emotions. Because we constantly seek signs, the earth, the world and society will provide them for us. When the signs are not examined properly, they make suggestions and paint pictures in our imaginations that will have to be resolved.

For example, when the media tells us of wars in the Middle East, unstable economies, joblessness in nations and moral decay, one is almost pulled into a position of hopelessness. With all these dangerous signs looming over us, what are we to do? It is evident that without any real direction and instruction, distractions are inevitable. What are distractions?

Distraction is:

D = **D**estiny
I = **I**nterfering
S = **S**ignals
T = **T**urning your
R = **R**esponses,
A = **A**ttention, and
C = **C**onsciousness to
T = **T**hings that
I = **I**ntentionally
O = **O**ppose your
N = **N**ext promotion

Distractions *are deliberate attempts to redirect your focus from the requirements of* vision *development and fulfillment*

4 Key elements:

- **Complications:** Difficult decisions
- **Confusion:** Too many choices
- **Complexity:** Unclear pictures
- **Changes:** Character challenges

Distractions can stem from many causes and have just as many objectives. I want to list some causes and their objectives.

Distractions Causes and Objectives

Lev 26:36 And upon them that are left alive of you I will send a faintness into their hearts in the lands of their enemies; and the sound of a shaken leaf shall chase them; and they shall flee, as fleeing from a sword; and they shall fall when none pursueth.

1. **Disobedience:** God calls resistance to the command an act of disobedience that grabs the hearts of people to give the impression that they are surrounded by their enemies. The sound of the rustling of the wind in the leaves gives the appearance that someone is chasing them and they will crumble when no one is pursuing.

Lev 26:37 And they shall fall one upon another, as it were before a sword, when none pursueth: and ye shall have no power to stand before your enemies.

2. Decisive actions: Lev 26:37 because of this relentless resistance the people will fall upon one another as if someone had smitten them with the sword and there will be no one pursuing. They will not be able to stand against the power of their enemies because of the fear that has captured their hearts.

Lev 26:38 And ye shall perish among the heathen, and the land of your enemies shall eat you up.

3. **Definite outcomes**: a picture of the ultimate ruin is displayed in **Lev 26:38**. There will be a total consumption in the land of your enemies. Fear will strip away any hope for future prosperity and security.

Lev 26:39 And they that are left of you shall pine away in their iniquity in your enemies' lands; and also in the iniquities of their fathers shall they pine away with them.

4. **Desolation: Lev 26:39** depicts that there will be a pinning away because of the presence of iniquity. This generational sin will cause a deterioration of the hope and the security of their nation.

This principle clearly states that all of the distractions above are destiny-interfering signals whose objective is to turn our responses, attention and consciousness to the things that will intentionally oppose our promotion and hinder our performance. This definition reminds us that there are deliberate attempts to redirect our focus away from any requirements necessary for vision development and fulfillment.

There are four elements that will accompany every moment of distraction:

1. **Complications:** the stress of difficult decisions.
2. **Confusion:** too many choices without any clarity of direction.
3. **Complexity:** of canvas full of unclear pictures.
4. **Changes:** character challenging experience this.

CHAPTER TWO

WHAT IS TERROR?

Phil 1:28 And in nothing terrified by your adversaries: which is to them an evident token of perdition, but to you of salvation, and that of God.

We must not allow the sudden onset of the presence of peace disturbing experiences to dictate a behavior pattern that would reflect the loss of our confidence. In this scripture, the Apostle Paul warns us that there is absolutely nothing that should create this subjective experience in our hearts. We must understand that we are dealing with an enemy named Satan, who has already been defeated. Therefore, whatever he challenges us with, however factual it may be, the truth is that we already have the victory.

1John 5:18 We know that whosoever is born of God sinneth not; but he that is begotten of God keepeth himself, and that wicked one toucheth him not.

The first thing we must consider is whether or not we are really born of God. After answering that question in the affirmative, we must separate ourselves from deliberate violations of the commands of God. We then have the responsibility of maintaining our position and strengthening our covenant with God. We must begin to rehearse the benefits, values and protective clauses implicit in this covenant. We must come to the conclusion that the enemy, however his strength is perceived, has no power to control our destinies.

1John 4:18 *There is no fear in love;*

but perfect love casteth out fear: because fear hath torment. He that feareth is not made perfect in love.

The Apostle John wants us to know that there is absolutely no room for fear in the heart of the believer that knows that God loves them. There is absolutely no way the love of God is insufficient to handle any opposition against His desire for you. It is inconceivable that God would call you to be a benefactor of His love and then torment you because of your decision to accept it.

The anxiety that one experiences is due to an underdeveloped picture of the provision and the protection of the love experience that one has with God. The presence of fear and its controlling force is evidence there is a lack of trust. What is trust?

Trust is:

T = **T**otal
R = **R**eliance
U = **U**pon
S = **S**criptural
T = **T**ruths

Trust is having complete reliance upon, without regard to any internal or external contingencies that could threaten your commitment to vision development and fulfillment

3 Key elements:

- **Confidence:** the assurance
- **Conviction:** the persuasion
- **Commitment:** the dedication

From this principle we can see that trust demands a complete and total reliance on scriptural truth. There can be no room for second-guessing the ability and the authority of God. We must be absolutely confident that God has never lost a battle and neither is He about to lose the one we are currently engaged in.

This principle reminds us that there must be a complete reliance upon this truth without regard to any internal or external contingencies that would attempt to threaten our commitment to our assignment. Heaven, the world and the inhabitants of the earth are banking on our consistency and our success.

Remember, the Apostle Paul told us that in nothing are we to allow terror to govern our behavior. What is terror?

Terror is a:

T = **T**hreatening and
E = **E**xasperating
R = **R**egistration of
R = **R**elentless
O = **O**pposition and
R = **R**uin

***Terror** is the force that attempts to control responses by introducing horrifying acts with life threatening consequences to hinder vision development and fulfillment*

3 Key elements:

- **Fright**
- **Fear**
- **Dread**

From this principle we can see that terror is the threatening and exasperating registration of relentless opposition and ruin. This definition reveals to us that terror is a force that tends to control our response by introducing horrifying acts that have life-threatening consequences.

This onslaught of attack creates a manifestation of the three key elements: fright, fear and dread.

There are several things that the force of terror creates in the minds of believers. Number one is a sense of being overwhelmed.

In one of those rare occasions when Israel's commitment and allegiance were in alignment with God they were actually a terror to their enemies. This is seen in Numbers 22:3.

> **Num 22:3** And Moab was sore afraid of the people, because they were many: and Moab was distressed because of the children of Israel.

The picture we see here is that of Israel's overwhelming presence of power against their enemy, which resulted in terror in the hearts of their opponent.

The second effect of terror on the believer is an ominous affect, illuminated in Job 18:11-14.

> **Job 18:11** ¶ Terrors shall make him afraid on every side, and shall drive him to his feet.
> **Job 18:12** His strength shall be hungerbitten, and destruction shall be ready at his side.
> **Job 18:13** It shall devour the strength

of his skin: even the firstborn of death shall devour his strength.

Job 18:14   His confidence shall be rooted out of his tabernacle, and it shall bring him to the king of terrors.

In verse 11 we see that terror wants to control you by surrounding you with its ominous presence. Terror wants you to have a sense of being consumed by its ominous presence.

Then terror, revealed in verse 13, creates a crippling effect because of its ominous presence. It states that terror will devour the strength of your skin. When we think about the human skin we think about protection from the environment. There are vital organs inside of our bodies that cannot be penetrated except the skin is breached. When the skin is consumed our protection is gone.

Finally, we see in verse 14 that terror is a confidence stripper. Whenever your confidence goes, your courage and your commitment also go. It is absolutely essential that our confidence remains secure. Our confidence is vital to our ability to stand in faith against the attacks of Satan and the environment. What is confidence?

Confidence is:

C = **C**omplete
O = **O**ptimism
N = **N**ecessary for
F = **F**avorable
I = **I**ncrease,
D = **D**ominion, and
E = **E**xcellence;
N = **N**egotiated by
C = **C**ourageous
E = **E**xpectation

> *Confidence is the courageous disposition obtained by absolute unfailing trust in the systems' successful historical accounts that support vision development and fulfillment*

3 Key elements:

- **Belief**
- **Assurance**
- **Certainty**

From this principle we can clearly see that confidence commands us to have and maintain complete   optimism.   This   disposition   is absolutely necessary for favorable increase and dominion. It is from this vantage point that we negotiate with courageous expectations.

The principle definition tells us that confidence is replete with a courageous disposition that is obtained by absolute, unfailing trust in the systems' successful historical accounts, that support vision development and fulfillment.

There are three key elements that must be present at every moment confidence is embraced: belief, assurance, and certainty.

Heb 10:35 Cast not away therefore your confidence, which hath great recompence of reward.

1John 5:14 And this is the confidence that we have in him, that, if we ask any thing according to his will, he heareth us:

1John 5:15 And if we know that he hear us, whatsoever we ask, we know that we have the petitions that we desired of him.

From these verses we can see that it is absolutely critical that we do not disregard our confidence. It will produce and provide for us great rewards. The Apostle John tells us that this confidence is defined by our knowledge that when we make a request of God, according to His will, He hears us. And, because we've asked according to His will and He does hear us, we know that the petition will be granted.

Now, let's go back to the ominous effects of terror.

The third position in its ominous effect of terror is a sense of being overcome, Psalms 73:19.

Ps 73:19 How are they [brought] into desolation, as in a moment! they are utterly consumed with terrors.

This verse reveals that there is an instant feeling of desolation to the degree that the terror has suddenly overcome you. With this fear and desolation there is the disintegration of hope. This forces us to panic and not trust the promises that God has made to us. There is a sense of abandonment.

The fourth position in the ominous effect of terror is obstinacy, depicted in **Proverbs 1:24-27**.

Prov 1:24 Because I have called, and ye refused; I have stretched out my hand, and no man regarded;

Prov 1:25 But ye have set at nought all my counsel, and would none of my reproof:

Prov 1:26 I also will laugh at your calamity; I will mock when your fear cometh;

Prov 1:27 When your fear cometh as desolation, and your destruction cometh as a whirlwind; when distress and anguish cometh upon you.

There are four consequences of obstinacy revealed in this paragraph.   First, truth is rejected. God says, "I called out to you but you refused; I stretched out my hand and you did not regard." Second, correction is resisted, from verse 25, "you disregarded all my counsel and you ignored my reproof."

Third, God is forced to reciprocate His responses to this obstinacy.   He states, "because you did not respond to me properly I am going to laugh at your calamities and mock when your fear comes."

The final threat that comes as a result of this obstinacy is consistent, relentless assaults.   He says fear comes as desolation and destruction as a whirldwind. In distress and anguish there is no escape.

In the face of these overwhelming odds, what are the weapons we can use against terror or terrorism? There is a powerful portrayal of principles that can be applied to the life of the believer today, found in Isaiah 54:11-17. We will study that in the next chapter.

I know that I may be treading on thin ice where biblical interpretation or application may be concerned. There are some who would read the writings of the prophets in the Old Testament and would conclude that many of the provisions in the promises made to Israel are not applicable to us today. I would agree that there does seem to be geographical and territorial benefits directly ascribed to those who were called Jews. However, I am convinced that in principle the promises were transferred to those New Testament believers who would come after them through Jesus Christ. We have an inheritance because we are the seed of Abraham, by faith in Christ Jesus.

Rom 4:13 For the promise, that he should be the heir of the world, was not to Abraham, or to his seed, through the law, but through the righteousness of faith.

Rom 4:16 Therefore it is of faith, that it might be by grace; to the end the promise might be sure to all the seed; not to that only which is of the law, but to that also which is of the faith of Abraham; who is the father of us all,

Heb 2:16 For verily he took not on him the nature of angels; but he took on him the seed of Abraham.

Rom 3:29 Is he the God of the Jews only? is he not also of the Gentiles? Yes, of the Gentiles also:

Rom 3:30 Seeing it is one God, which shall justify the circumcision by faith, and uncircumcision through faith.

The Apostle Paul reveals to us God's desire to bring His righteousness to all of humanity, not on the basis of the law, but through faith. He further asserts that this new position is of faith, so that it might be by grace, to make sure that the benefit of righteousness by faith extends itself to all of the seed of Abraham. This position was guaranteed to all the seed because Jesus took upon Himself the nature of Abraham, not that of angels. He reminds those Jews that He's not a God of the Jews only but also of the

Gentiles. Therefore, as the Jews were justified by faith because of their circumcision, the Gentiles, because of their uncircumcision, would be justified through faith.

Gal 3:16 Now to Abraham and his seed were the promises made. He saith not, And to seeds, as of many; but as of one, And to thy seed, which is Christ.

Gal 3:26 For ye are all the children of God by faith in Christ Jesus.

Gal 3:27 For as many of you as have been baptized into Christ have put on Christ.

Gal 3:28 There is neither Jew nor Greek, there is neither bond nor free, there is neither male nor female: for ye are all one in Christ Jesus.

Gal 3:29 And if ye be Christ's, then are ye Abraham's seed, and heirs according to the promise.

In the book of Galatians he tells the believers of Galatia that these promises were made to Abraham and his seed, not seeds as of many; but one seed, which the Apostle Paul affirms is Christ. He further asserts that we are all the children of God by faith, in His righteous principles, because of Jesus Christ. And, because of baptism, we have put on this Christ.

In Christ there is no longer a distinction where the principle of faith and righteousness are concerned between the Jew or the Greek, the slave or the free, or in the male or the female. He asserts that we are all benefactors of this principle of righteousness through faith because of Jesus Christ. He says that if we are in Christ, then we are Abraham's seed and heirs according to the promise made to Abraham.

Gal 3:14 That the blessing of Abraham might come on the Gentiles through Jesus Christ; that we might receive the promise of the Spirit through faith.

Finally, the apostle reveals to us how we can make the assertion and claim that these promises, in principle, were transferred to the Gentiles in faith through Jesus Christ. He says that we receive the promise of the spirit through faith. This is not based upon a biological or geographical inheritance but a commitment of God to the Gentiles granted by insertion into the body through Jesus Christ on the principle of faith and righteousness.

CHAPTER THREE

WHAT ARE OUR WEAPONS AGAINST TERROR?
Isaiah 54:11-17

There are many forms of terror the enemy will use against the believer. In order to form a successful counter attack, we must know what we possess in our arsenal. First, there is comfort while unstable conditions challenge us.

Isa 54:11 ¶ O thou afflicted, tossed with tempest, and not comforted, behold, I will lay thy stones with fair colours, and lay thy foundations with sapphires.

This verse tells us that we can be comforted while afflicted and tossed with the relentless torrent of societal upheaval. God will secure our foundations with costly stones.

Second, there is promise for problems, depicted in verse 12.

Isa 54:12   And I will make thy windows of agates, and thy gates of carbuncles, and all thy borders of pleasant stones.

When we look through the windows of our circumstances we don't see calamity, confusion and chaos. We see gates of costly jewels and precious stones.   God wants to change our perspective on the situation.

Third, there is instruction for our ignorance, depicted in verse 13.

Isa 54:13 And all thy children shall be taught of the LORD; and great shall be the peace of thy children.

Our children will be taught of the Lord and the result of that instruction will be protection and peace for our children. We must remember that no matter what we're going through, there will always be spiritual security granted to our progeny and legacy.

Fourth, there will be protection from fear, depicted in verse 14.

Isa 54:14 In righteousness shalt thou be established: thou shalt be far from oppression; for thou shalt not fear: and from terror; for it shall not come near thee.

He reminds us that in righteousness we will be established. Remember the definition of righteousness: *God had some things in His heart concerning me. He said them out of His mouth and they became a reality in His world. When I say out of my mouth the things that God said concerning me and believe in my heart that they shall come to pass, they will be a reality in my world.* This is the principle that I must use to become established in the midst of whatever terror-filled attack I'm experiencing. With this disposition, I will be removed from oppression. The foreboding presence of fear and terror will not come near me. My righteousness will speak for me.

Fifth, threats will be without substance. This is depicted in verse 15.

> **Isa 54:15**   Behold, they shall surely gather together, but not by me: whosoever shall gather together against thee shall fall for thy sake.

There will be the appearance of an overwhelming gathering against you, but, God says, "It will not be by Me that they have gathered", and, "whoever is gathering against you will fall by your side."

Sixth is sovereignty for insecurity, as revealed in verse 16.

> **Isa 54:16**   Behold, I have created the smith that bloweth the coals in the fire, and that bringeth forth an instrument for his work; and I have created the waster to destroy.

This verse can be a bit alarming without some in-depth understanding of what has transpired. It appears that God is responsible for creating what this verse calls the waster or the destroyer. You must understand that God did create Lucifer, the light bearer. Lucifer's fall from glory transformed him into Satan. The light bearer is now the thief, the killer and the destroyer.

> **John 10:10** The thief cometh not, but for to steal, and to kill, and to destroy: I am come that they might have life, and that they might have it more abundantly.

In his original state, Lucifer was created by God. But, the perversion of his original design created Satan. Therefore, his threats against you are without substance. You are protected by your Father, God Almighty.

Seventh, invincibility from invasion, as depicted in verse 17.

> **Isa 54:17** No weapon that is formed against thee shall prosper; and every tongue that shall rise against thee in judgment thou shalt condemn. This is the heritage of the servants of the LORD, and

their righteousness is of me, saith the
LORD.

The prophet wants us to see that there is no
weapon, however formidable, that can form
against us that will prosper. Mind you, he did
not say an attack will not come, nor, that the
enemy will not rise up against us. The
assurance that we have is that, no matter how
challenging the circumstances are, they will
have no real effect on our substance or on our
success.

Let's review the keys in the weapons that we
can use to fight against terror and terrorism.
Remember, the prophet Isaiah says that God
wants to give us comfort while we are in the
midst of the most unstable and unsettling times.
Second, he wants us to know that there is a
promise for every moment of every problem that
we encounter. Third, there is the comfort of
instruction for the ignorance that has enveloped
us. Fourth, we get protection from the fear that
is created by the circumstances that are trying
to surround us. Fifth, he reveals to us that
these threats against us are without substance.
Sixth, he reminds us that his sovereignty is to
protect our insecurity. Finally, there is

invincibility against every moment of the threat of the reality of invasion.

CHAPTER FOUR

WHAT IS OUR SECURITY FROM TERROR?
1Peter 3:8-15

Security is the

S = **S**afeguard
E = **E**xperienced being
C = **C**overed by
U = **U**nbeatable,
R = **R**esponsible and
I = **I**ndomitable
T = **T**enderness that
Y = **Y**ields success

***Security** is the comfort, confidence, and safety one experiences from solid relationships that support vision development and fulfillment*

3 Key elements:

- **Comfort**
- **Confidence**
- **Safety**

From this principle, we can see that security safeguards our experiences with a covering that is unbeatable, responsible and tender. Yet, it has a toughness that creates an opportunity to yield success.

This principle definition reminds us that security is comfort, confidence and safety experienced from solid relationships. There is absolutely no relationship more solid than the relationship between a believer and his eternal Father.

There are three key elements, consistent with every experience of security:comfort, confidence and safety.

The security that we can experience in the presence of any horrifying experience has been captured by the Apostle Peter in 1Peter 3:8-15.

1Pet 3:8 ¶ Finally, be ye all of one mind, having compassion one of another, love as brethren, be pitiful, be courteous:

1Pet 3:9 Not rendering evil for evil, or railing for railing: but contrariwise blessing; knowing that ye are thereunto called, that ye should inherit a blessing.

1Pet 3:10 For he that will love life, and see good days, let him refrain his tongue from evil, and his lips that they speak no guile:

1Pet 3:11 Let him eschew evil, and do good; let him seek peace, and ensue it.

1Pet 3:12 For the eyes of the Lord are over the righteous, and his ears are open unto their prayers: but the face of the Lord is against them that do evil.

1Pet 3:13 And who is he that will harm you, if ye be followers of that which is good?

1Pet 3:14 But and if ye suffer for righteousness' sake, happy are ye: and be not afraid of their terror, neither be troubled;

1Pet 3:15 But sanctify the Lord God in your hearts: and be ready always to give an answer to every man that asketh you a reason of the hope that is in you with meekness and fear:

First, the apostle tells us that there is a compassion that we need to have for each other that provides a sense of security like nothing else can. In verse 8 he states that we need to have a singleness of mind that moves us to have compassion for each other and to be courteous and deeply respectful of each other.

Second, the apostle tells us that we must learn to respond and not to react, as depicted in verse 9. We must cease to react to the presence of evil with evil forces. We must dispense with the senseless debates that further separate us and threaten our security. We must choose to take the high road. When we do, we will inherit a blessing from our Father.

Third, the apostle tells us that we must activate speech control, as depicted in verse 10. He says that if we have a fondness for life and want to see good days, then we must learn to control what comes out of our mouths. We must remove duplicity from our hearts so that our mouths can represent our integrity.

Fourth, the apostle tells us that our motivation must be properly displayed. Look at verse 11. We must shy away from evil and purpose to do well. We must always be in pursuit of peace and capture it.

Peace is the:

P = **P**ower,
E = **E**xperience
A = **A**uthority and
C = **C**onfidence to
E = **E**xecute

Peace is the tranquil state one realizes in anticipation of the manifestation of the resources required to complete the visions' demands

3 Key elements:

- **Calmness**
- **Coolness**
- **Composure**

From this principle we can see that peace is the presentation of power experience authority and confidence. This gives us the ability to execute with a correct expectation. The principle definition tells us that peace is the tranquil state that anyone can realize as one anticipates the manifestation of the resources required to complete the demands of vision.

There are three key elements that are present at every moment and second of peace: calmness, coolness and composure.

The fifth is revealed in verse 12 , a divine covering. The apostle wants us to know that we are under the umbrella of the ever observant, protective eyes of God. As we stand in righteousness His ear is open to our prayers. Righteousness is the foundation by which the words we utter causes heaven to respond in a favorable way. He reminds us that the face of the Lord is against those who do evil.

Number seven is self-sacrifice, depicted in verse 14. The apostle reminds us that if for whatever reason we are experiencing an injustice because of righteousness we are to display an attitude of gratitude. Because the challenge has come to us because of our right standing with God, we don't have to be afraid of any terror that it creates or trouble that results from it.

Finally, we must embrace a sanctified heart. This is depicted in verse 15. The apostle tells us we must purpose to sanctify the Lord God in our hearts.

You must understand that out of the abundance of the heart, the mouth speaks. The heart must be protected with all diligence. We must make sure that the contents of our heart meets the approval of heaven at all times. When this is accomplished, we are always ready to give to everyone that asks the reason of the hope that is within us.

Let's review the eight keys that provide us with security from terror:

- Compassion For Each Other
- Responding Not Reacting
- Speech Control
- Proper Motivation
- Divine Covering
- Divine Protection

- Self Sacrifice
- Sanctified Heart

Meditating on these keys will allow us to have confidence in God, and the tools we need to have security from terror.

CHAPTER FIVE

REMOVING THE APPREHENSION
Philippians 4:6-9

Phil 4:6 Be careful for nothing; but in every thing by prayer and supplication with thanksgiving let your requests be made known unto God.

Phil 4:7 And the peace of God, which

passeth all understanding, shall keep your hearts and minds through Christ Jesus.

Phil 4:8 Finally, brethren, whatsoever things are true, whatsoever things are honest, whatsoever things are just, whatsoever things are pure, whatsoever things are lovely, whatsoever things are of good report; if there be any virtue, and if there be any praise, think on these things.

Phil 4:9 Those things, which ye have both learned, and received, and heard, and seen in me, do: and the God of peace shall be with you.

The last two to three years of my life have been very trying. I've had two major surgeries. The first was a severe back injury that, if not caught in time, would have left me paralyzed from the waist down. The second was due to cancer, discovered in my prostate gland. Were it not for the presence of God, both of these announcements could have created the most apprehension I have ever had in my life as a believer.

However, I was armed with the tools that I am about to share with you. These tools caused me to successfully navigate through the unsettling waters and the raging currents that were attempting to dash my hopes on the rocks of despair. I found those tools in Phillipians 4:6-9. There are things in this brief paragraph the Apostle Paul wants us to internalize that help dampen despair.

First of all, we must decide to trust God. We display this trust by controlling our passion and redirecting our focus.

He states in verse 6 that we are not to be careful. That is, we are not to be filled with anxiety about anything. We must make a decision to let our prayer and supplication be registered in heaven, with thanksgiving, revealing to others that we made our request known to God.

Second, the apostle says to be sensitive to the divine intervention this is depicted in verse 7. We are reminded that there is a peace that comes from God that is quite capable of keeping our hearts and our minds.

I cannot begin to tell you how tempting it was for me to discuss with myself and others the circumstances surrounding both of these prognoses. The better judgment of the power and the promises of God allowed me to keep my heart locked into the promises that God made, thus supporting and not nullifying the benefits of those promises. Through the power and promises of God, I was able to also keep my mind.

Let me share with you what I believe the Holy Spirit says the mind is.

Mind is:

M = **M**ental
I = **I**nsight to
N = **N**egotiate
D = **D**ominion

> ***Mind*** *is the storehouse of the intelligence factors that empowers our ability to alter circumstances and situations that can hinder or support the demands for vision development and fulfillment*

5 Key elements:

- **The storehouse of memory**
- **The incubation chamber of imagination**
- **The processor of thoughts**
- **The location of all logic**
- **The reservoir for reasoning**

From this principle we can see that the mind is the mental insight or acuity to negotiate dominion and, in some cases, defeat. The principle definition says that it is the storehouse of the intelligence factors that empowers our ability to alter every set of circumstances and situations that can hinder or support vision demands.

From the key elements you can see how important it is to support healthy mental functions. The mind is the key in the acquisition and manifestation of victory over fear and the silence of terrorism. It is therefore the peace of God that must be placed in all of the faculties of the mind to guarantee victory all the time.

The third thing the Apostle Paul wants us to note is that we must clean up our thought life. The mind must be developed. In verse 8 we are shown which things we are to think about: those things that are true, honest, just, pure, lovely and of a good report. He says if there's any virtue or qualities that we would deem notable or noteworthy or praise we must think on these things.

Finally, the apostle tells us that we must duplicate the example of divine leadership in our personal lives. Look at verse 9. He says the things that we have learned, received, heard and seen in those who instructed us, we must duplicate.

Let's review once again the four principles that will assist us in the removal of apprehension:

- Decide to trust God!
- Be sensitive to divine intervention!
- Clean up your thought life!
- Duplicate the example of divine leadership in your personal life!

CHAPTER SIX

ARRESTING THE ANXIETY
Mark 4:35-41

Mark 4:35 ¶ And the same day, when the even was come, he saith unto them, Let us pass over unto the other side.

Mark 4:36 And when they had sent away the multitude, they took him even as he was in the ship. And there were also with him other little ships.

Mark 4:37   And there arose a great storm of wind, and the waves beat into the ship, so that it was now full.

Mark 4:38   And he was in the hinder part of the ship, asleep on a pillow: and they awake him, and say unto him, Master, carest thou not that we perish?

Mark 4:39   And he arose, and rebuked the wind, and said unto the sea, Peace, be still. And the wind ceased, and there was a great calm.

Mark 4:40   And he said unto them, Why are ye so fearful? how is it that ye have no faith?

Mark 4:41   And they feared exceedingly, and said one to another, What manner of man is this, that even the wind and the sea obey him?

It is fairly obvious that we will not be able to master the skills, the tools and the techniques for overcoming fearful situations if we are not able to arrest the moments of anxiety that are produced because of the fear. In order to arrest these maniacal, menacing and unsettling forces, there are some keys that we will have to internalize.

I would like to draw your attention back to Mark 4:35-41. The apostle captures the scene on the banks of Galilee where Jesus is giving parting instructions to His disciples. This paragraph reveals seven powerful keys that, if used properly, will assist us in arresting every moment of anxiety that is created by the onset of circumstances that induce fear.

First of all, the apostle tells us that we must follow instructions. Look in verse 35. We must activate the power of giving and receiving directions. The Master simply says, "let us pass over to the other side." The disciples certainly did not anticipate any conflict with such a simple set of instructions. Even if the difficulty is not anticipated we cannot allow the circumstances to frustrate our obedience. There can not be any excuse for not following the instruction.

Second, protect the people. We must know that others are equally at risk. In verse 36 He reveals to us that in addition to us receiving instructions, there are others that are equally affected. Sometimes our vision is so myopic we cannot clearly see the others that are depending upon our faithfulness. The Apostle Mark wants us to understand that when Jesus instructed His disciples He wanted them to know that there were others that would be affected by their focus. The slightest deviation could create catastrophic circumstances for those whose only hope may be our consistent success. Therefore, our commitment to the instructions is crucial.

The third thing he writes is to expect challenges. We must anticipate the source of the storms of life, depicted in verse 37. We must learn to anticipate the storms of life. I wrote a book called *Sailing Through The Storms* of life. My daughter-in-law, Deria, says that it is crisis management size. The book is small enough to fit into your pocket or purse. You should get your hands on a copy of it. We cannot go through this life without the realization that there will be some difficulties. This realization demands that we make preparations because problems and pain are impossible to avoid.

The fourth thing the apostle wants us to understand is that we must sense our security, found in verse 38. Know who is on board with you! We must come to terms with the knowledge that we know that the Word of God is on board with us. I love this story. It says that Jesus was in the hinder part of the boat asleep. When you think you are sailing through a storm and there is no hope on your boat, you must re-examine the situation. Jesus is committed to you. He will never leave you, nor forsake you. He is on the boat.

The fifth point the apostle wants us to see is that we must believe the best, found in verse 39. We can do that when we know the power of the one who has ultimate responsibility. I know that Jesus is quite capable of dealing with any set of circumstances life throws your way. Remember, Jesus is the Son of God, the Word of God and God Himself. Once you get the Word of God into your heart, you have God on board with you.

The sixth thing the apostle wants us to see is that we must face our fear, depicted in verse 40. We must be prepared to address our failure. His response to their hopelessness was, "Why is it that you have no faith and why are you so fearful?" It was a challenge to the Master that, after having taught them all day long, fear continued to rule the hearts of His pupils, not faith.

The final thing that he wants us to see in this paragraph is that we must examine our expectations. This is clearly depicted in verse 41. We must not justify our ineptness. To compliment the Son of God because we failed in our ability to respond like He desires is mere flattery, not honor. This flattery suggests that the lesson they should have learned eluded them again.   The Master is much more interested in knowing that we have learned from our errors and are prepared to capitalize the next time.

CHAPTER SEVEN

TURNING OFF THE ALARM
JOHN 11:17-26

John 11:17 ¶ Then when Jesus came, he found that he had lain in the grave four days already.

John 11:18 Now Bethany was nigh unto Jerusalem, about fifteen furlongs off:

John 11:19 And many of the Jews came to Martha and Mary, to comfort them concerning their brother.

John 11:20 Then Martha, as soon as she heard that Jesus was coming, went and met him: but Mary sat still in the house.

John 11:21 Then said Martha unto Jesus, Lord, if thou hadst been here, my brother had not died.

John 11:22 But I know, that even now, whatsoever thou wilt ask of God, God will give it thee.

John 11:23 Jesus saith unto her, Thy brother shall rise again.

John 11:24 Martha saith unto him, I know that he shall rise again in the resurrection at the last day.

John 11:25 Jesus said unto her, I am the resurrection, and the life: he that believeth in me, though he were dead, yet shall he live:

John 11:26 And whosoever liveth and believeth in me shall never die. Believest thou this?

Life can deal some pretty difficult cards to us. I am reminded of the experience of the death of

Jesus' friend Lazarus.   Jesus' communication with the disciples would indicate His lack of concern for the impending doom of his friend. You must remember that Jesus is the Word of God and He is omniscient and has the ability in the spirit realm to be omnipresent. We must be real careful not to judge a moment in time to be isolated and off limits to His eternity. As it turned out, Lazarus died. John 11:17-26 captures the aftermath of Lazarus' death.

There are nine keys that stand out when we examine this whole ordeal. The Apostle John wants us to know that nothing is impossible. This is depicted in verse 17.

First, we must not allow any situation to determine the outcome. When Jesus had come to the grave of Lazarus it was discovered that he had been dead for four days. To anybody else panic would have set in, fear would have grabbed them and, the moment would have been terrifying. Remember, we are dealing with the *Son of God*.

The second thing the apostle wants us to see is that distance is not a threat to the outcome. It means nothing! This is depicted in verse 18. We must come to the conclusion that distance is not a threat to the outcome we expect.   It is revealed here that Jerusalem was quite a distance away from where they were located. This distance accounted for the fact that he was dead for four days.

Third, the apostle wants us to understand that we must be aware of the wrong intentions of well wishers. Look at verse 19. And, we must not be distracted by the sympathy of well-wishers. The apostle reveals that many Jews came to comfort Mary and Martha concerning the death of their brother, not the resurrection of their brother.

The fourth thing the apostle wants us to see here is that a demand for directions must be insisted upon. This is depicted in verse 20. We must learn to respond immediately to the presence of help. This verse reveals that as soon as Martha heard that Jesus was coming, she immediately got up to go and meet with Him. The immediacy of her presence was a demand for help.

The fifth thing the apostle wants us to see is that we must be prepared to have ignorance challenged. We must address the crisis head on. This is depicted in verse 21. Martha cries out in an accusatory way to Jesus, "If you had not been so insensitive my brother would still be alive." You must understand that this is a purely human response. It is not an indictment, at least in her mind, against the integrity of the Son of God. Martha is speaking from a disadvantage of fear and grief. She has some basic knowledge of Jesus' ability. However, this basic knowledge is not enough to eradicate the despondency created by the grief at the loss of her brother and at the fear of facing days without him.

The sixth thing the apostle wants us to see is that we must speak our success. State your confidence in spite of the circumstances! This is depicted in verse 22. Immediately after that accusation, Martha retorts, "I know that whatever You ask God for, He will respond favorably to You." We must learn to state our confidence in spite of our circumstances. Here we see Martha grasping at straws. It is common, when desperation sets in, to make a plea for a miracle outside of the faith required to support it. A plea like this one is not unusual. Fear can produce some amazing requests.

The seventh thing the apostle wants us to see is that we must picture the performance, depicted in verse 23. We must prepare for the supernatural to invade the natural areas of our lives. Jesus responds to her, "your brother will rise again." Jesus deals with Martha's act of desperation by telling her that He is capable of immediately producing what she requested. However, this is beyond Martha's ability to comprehend. Her perception of His ability is limited to her knowledge of Him. It is evident that the crises in our lives cannot be mastered by the limited knowledge that we have of the Word of God.

The eighth thing is the demand for perfect perceptions, depicted in verse 24. Prepare to have your ignorance corrected. Martha says, "I know my brother will arise again in the resurrection." This is a clear indication of her ignorance of whom it is she is addressing. This element of faith requires us to, in spite of the circumstances, display confidence in the Word of God to produce what He said. This concept is difficult for the natural mind to do on a normal basis. When you couple a crisis with an abnormal experience, it becomes almost impossible to function at this level of faith. Without the ability to function at this level of faith in the present arena of disaster, fear will always respond.

Finally, we must learn from Jesus that we must accentuate our assignment. This is depicted in verses 25-26. Clearly, Jesus was prepared to deal with unbelief's challenge to the miraculous. Jesus reminds Martha, "I am the resurrection and the life. There is no situation that is impossible for Me to address with a favorable outcome." Jesus challenged her belief system.

It was difficult for Martha to internalize the concept that Jesus was capable of doing what the word says He can do. She thought that this was a prophetic expectation. In spite of this, she hoped that this would take place now. The death of her brother and the desperation at Jesus' absence would not allow her to understand that her request could be fulfilled.

Let's review the nine keys required by faith to turn off the alarming situations that create fear:

- Do not allow any situation to determine the outcome!
- Distance is not a threat to the outcome!
- Be aware of wrong intentions!
- Insist on a demand for directions!
- Be prepared to have your ignorance challenged!
- Speak your success!
- Picture the performance!
- Demand perfect perceptions!
- Accentuate the assignment!

CHAPTER EIGHT

KNOW THE REMEDY FOR FEAR

2Tim 1:7 For God hath not given us the spirit of fear; but of power, and of love, and of a sound mind.

As we have examined all seven points of the challenging circumstances that create and surround our lives with fear and terror, it is now time to look at the remedy that must be applied to all of the circumstances.

The first thing we need to do is picture the potential of the power and the love of God. This is depicted in **2Tim 1:7**. Here the Apostle Paul is reminding us that we have not been given a spirit (the personification of a demon presence) that invokes fear in us.

This verse reminds me of a story that occurred in the Old Testament. It appears that one of the kings of Israel was confronted by serious opposition to the security of the nation. But against the council and the will of God he wanted to engage the confrontation. Little did he know that if he persisted with his plan, it would be ultimate destruction because of sinister spiritual intervention. The word of God says that a demon spirit of deception would create an opportunity for disaster. It is clear from this paragraph in 1Kings 22:20-22 that God was not the author of this deception.

> **1Kings 22:20**   And the LORD said, Who shall persuade Ahab, that he may go up and fall at Ramothgilead? And one said on this manner, and another said on that manner.

1Kings 22:21 And there came forth a spirit, and stood before the LORD, and said, I will persuade him.

1Kings 22:22 And the LORD said unto him, Wherewith? And he said, I will go forth, and I will be a lying spirit in the mouth of all his prophets. And he said, Thou shalt persuade him, and prevail also: go forth, and do so.

Let's go back to Paul's statement in 2Timothy 1:7 and see if we can gain some greater insight.

2Tim 1:7 For God hath not given us the spirit of fear; but of power, and of love, and of a sound mind.

But, we have been given power, love and a sound mind. Paul says that there are three things that have been imparted to every believer. These three elements are sufficient to dispel the spirit of fear and its awful effect. First of all, let's deal with the element of power. What is power?

Power is:

P = **P**osition,
O = **O**pportunity,
W = **W**isdom,
E = **E**xperience, and
R = **R**esources

*Power is the ability to influence, command,
and control events for the presentation of
purpose and the realization of destiny
for vision development and fulfillment*

3 Key elements:

- **Influence**
- **Command**
- **Control**

This principle tells us that no matter what it looks like, we are in a better position, we have a better set of circumstances and that wisdom surrounds us. God's expectation is for us to tap into the resources available to us. The principle definition states that we have the ability to influence, command and control events for the presentation of purpose and the realization of destiny.

There are three keys that we need operate in a position of power. They are influence, command and control.

There is also a second definition of power I want to share with you that is realized after the first one is internalized.

Power is:

P = **P**otential
O = **O**perating
W = **W**ithout
E = **E**xperiencing
R = **R**estraint

> ***Power*** *is the ability to release potential to influence the development and fulfillment of vision*

3 Key elements:

- **Ability:** faculty
- **Influence:** effectiveness
- **Control:** management

This second "power" principle tells us that there is potential on the inside of us that can cause us to operate without experiencing any restraint at all. Once you realize that you are in position, you possess unlimited wisdom and opportunities. From God's perspective, heaven is behind you and the earth's resources are available to you. You cannot fail. At this point, every restraint has now been lifted. Therefore, the principle definition confirms that we have the ability to release this potential to influence the fulfillment of the expected vision.

The final thing in this verse the apostle wants us to comprehend is that we have been equipped with a sound mind. What is a sound mind?

Sound is the:

S = **S**olid,
O = **O**pportunistic,
U = **U**nimpaired,
N = **N**egotiable, and
D = **D**ependable

> ***Sound*** *is the healthy, sensible and reliable state of your design to develop and accomplish vision demands*

3 Key elements:
- **Healthy:** unimpaired
- **Sensible:** reasonable
- **Reliable:** trustworthy

This principle reveals to us that when we function from a position of soundness, there is stability. We are projected from a solid foundation. This position allows us to see that the opportunities are greater than the opposition. The challenge no longer renders us hopeless. This soundness gives us a greater ability to negotiate a better outcome. We now prove our dependability to those who have enlisted our service.

The principle definition says that this is a healthy, sensible and reliable state encoded in our design. This now provides us the ability to develop and to accomplish the visions' demands. With this thought in mind, no set of circumstances should invoke the spirit of fear. How does the mind support this position of strength? Let's revisit the definition of the mind.

Mind is:

M = **M**ental
I = **I**nsight to
N = **N**egotiate
D = **D**ominion

__Mind__ is the storehouse of the intelligence factors that empowers our ability to alter *circumstances and situations that can hinder or support the demands for vision development and fulfillment*

5 Key elements:

- **The storehouse of memory**
- **The incubation chamber of imagination**
- **The processor of thoughts**
- **The location of all logic**
- **The reservoir for reasoning**

This principle tells us that the mind is the mental insight to develop and negotiate the dominion we desire to see. But, an unstable mind will negotiate our defeat. The instability of the mind is a result of bad programming. However, when the mind is programmed properly, faith can be discharged. The Scripture tells us that we can take on the supernatural ability of Christs' mind.

1Cor 2:16 For who hath known the mind of the Lord, that he may instruct him? But we have the mind of Christ.

Knowing that we have the opportunity to take on the mind of Christ is sufficient to eradicate any force of negativity attempting to invoke the spirit of fear. We must know that Christ had victory in the mental arena. If He did not have this mental victory, it never would have manifested itself in His natural environment.

The principle definition tells us that the mind is the storehouse. This is where the intelligence that empowers our ability to adjust our thinking is housed. This intelligence helps us alter the circumstances and situations that can hinder vision development. We must do everything we can to protect the way information enters into our beings.

Since we released the first key at the beginning of this chapter, let's review it. The first thing we need to do is picture the potential of the power and the love of God.

The second key in the remedy for fear is positioned with power. Psalms 91:1-5:

Ps 91:1 ¶ He that dwelleth in the secret place of the most High shall abide under the shadow of the Almighty.

Ps 91:2 I will say of the LORD, He is my refuge and my fortress: my God; in him will I trust.

Ps 91:3 Surely he shall deliver thee from the snare of the fowler, and from the noisome pestilence.

Ps 91:4 He shall cover thee with his feathers, and under his wings shalt thou trust: his truth shall be thy shield and buckler.

Ps 91:5 Thou shalt not be afraid for the terror by night; nor for the arrow that flieth by day;

The psalmist wants us to see that there is security connected with our understanding that we are sitting in the secret place of the Most High. This is depicted in verse 1.

Ps 91:1 ¶ He that dwelleth in the secret place of the most High shall abide under the shadow of the Almighty.

I like the idea that the psalmist refers to this as the secret place. The Word of God says that the secret things belong to the Lord and the things that are revealed to us belong to us, and our children, that we may do all the words of the law. There are some things that the forces of darkness do not know about God, or about us.   There is a level of security that we can experience knowing that this is off limits to those forces.

Secondly,   the   psalmist   wants   us   to

understand that there is safety that has to do with the fortress that surrounds us when we trust. This is depicted in verse 2.

Ps 91:2 I will say of the LORD, He is my refuge and my fortress: my God; in him will I trust.

This passage paints a picture of the city, protected by the walls of a great fortress. Nothing is able to penetrate the walls of this fortress, which causes the inhabitants of the city to feel safe and live without fear. When God becomes your fortress, your mind, will and emotions are protected from the attack of fear.

Third, the psalmist wants us to see that there is an ability to escape. This is depicted in verse 3.

Ps 91:3 Surely he shall deliver thee from the snare of the fowler, and from the noisome pestilence.

God can deliver us from the snare of anything that is trying to trap us. Make no mistake about it, these negative circumstances that surround us are here on purpose. If we trust God, He is able to set a course that will navigate us through life, avoiding every snare the enemy lays for us.

The fourth thing the psalmist wants us to see is that there is a shielding protection depicted in verse 4.

Ps 91:4 He shall cover thee with his feathers, and under his wings shalt thou trust: his truth shall be thy shield and buckler.

God will cover us with the feathers of His wings as we trust Him. He will be that which stands between us and destruction.

The fifth thing He wants us to see is that because of His strength we don't have to be afraid of any terror or weapons formed against us. This is depicted in verse 5.

Ps 91:5 Thou shalt not be afraid for the terror by night; nor for the arrow that flieth by day;

It is amazing how the presence of darkness can invoke fear because of prior programming. The Bible says that men loved darkness rather than light because their deeds are evil. Many of the horror movies we watched as children (and, unfortunately, many of our children are watching today) created an uneasy foreboding of the presence of evil. So, whenever we hear about a dark day, there is this fear that is automatically associated with this picture. Isn't it comforting to know that the terror of darkness can no longer threaten us? There may be arrows flying but they will not penetrate our person.

The third key in the remedy for fear is to have a righteous resolve. This is depicted in Psalms 3:6.

Ps 3:6 I will not be afraid of ten thousands of people, that have set *themselves* against me round about.

We must gravitate to the position that no matter how many forces there seem to be against our efforts, we will not be afraid. Take confidence that God will drop them by your side. It doesn't matter how many fall by your side or the number of them who set themselves against you, fear must not grab you.

The fourth key in the remedy for fear is their fortitude depicted in Psalms 27:1-3.

Ps 27:1 ¶ *A Psalm* of David. The LORD *is* my light and my salvation; whom shall I fear? the LORD *is* the strength of my life; of whom shall I be afraid?

Ps 27:2 When the wicked, *even* mine enemies and my foes, came upon me to eat up my flesh, they stumbled and fell.

Ps 27:3 Though an host should encamp against me, my heart shall not fear: though war should rise against me, in this *will* I *be* confident.

David reminds us that God is our light and our salvation.

Light is:

L = **L**asting
I = **I**nsight,
G = **G**ood judgment and
H = **H**eaven inspired
T = **T**ruth

Light is the ability to clearly see the intent and understand the process by which methodical productivity and harmony will produce accomplishment and vision fulfillment

3 Key elements:

ᕦ **Clarity**
ᕦ **Enlightenment**
ᕦ **Brilliance**

This principle in the remedy for fear reveals to us that there is lasting insight, good judgment and heavenly inspired truth that must guide us every moment we are involved in a conflict or crisis. We must rest assured that this light is based upon Heaven inspired truth.

This principle definition says light is the ability to clearly see the intent and understand the process by methodical and productive harmony. This will produce the successful accomplishment of vision development and fulfillment.

David wants us to understand that when the Lord is your light and the presence of darkness has been lifted, there is no need to be afraid. He can now become the strength of your life.

Who is able to stand against God? Whenever your enemies come to strip you of your coverage they will stumble and fall. Even if a host of them gather against you, your heart must not harbor moments of fear. Even if there is an all out assault against your character, your name and your resources, you must maintain your confidence. Do not let fear dictate your response.

The fifth principle in the remedy for fear reveals to us our incredible stability, and is found in Psalms 46:2.

Ps 46:2   Therefore will not we fear, though the earth be removed, and though the mountains be carried into the midst of the sea;

David wants us to see that the whole earth may be unstable and the mountains could slip into the sea, but fear must not grab him. The mountains here could suggest the places over our hope and our confidence.

In recent times, here in the United States and in other nations around the world, financial institutions are crumbling, political regimes are toppling and global peace is threatened. We must not allow the circumstances to carry us to a place of panic. We will not fear.

The sixth principle in the remedy for fear reveals total trust, depicted in Psalms 112:7.

Ps 112:7   He shall not be afraid of evil tidings: his heart is fixed, trusting in the LORD.

David says that this disposition of total trust is based upon a heart that has been fixed or settled in the confidence of God. With this kind of confidence no evil tidings, however threatening, can create the sensation of fear in this heart. Absolute trust in God is essential to eradicating the foreboding presence of fear and its dictating our course of action. What is trust?

Trust is:

T = **T**otal
R = **R**eliance
U = **U**pon
S = **S**criptural
T = **T**ruths

> ***Trust*** *is complete reliance upon, without regard to any internal or external contingencies that could threaten your commitment to vision development and fulfillment*

3 Key elements:

- **Confidence:** the assurance
- **Conviction:** the persuasion
- **Commitment:** the dedication

This principle reveals to us that trust is complete and absolute reliance or confidence in Scriptural truth. This concept of trust commands us to accept the Word of God as the final authority and voice concerning the circumstances of our lives. The principle definition says that it is essential that a complete reliance be placed upon the Word of God without any regard to either external or internal contingencies. We must not allow any circumstances to affect our commitment to vision development and fulfillment.

In order to be able to trust at this level the one thing that is required is truth. We must conclude that the Word of God is truth. We must not believe that it contains truth, but that it is truth. Without truth as our solid foundation, total trust cannot be experienced. What is truth?

Truth is the:

T = **T**otally
R = **R**eliable,
U = **U**nadulterated,
T = **T**rustworth, and
H = **H**onest report

***Truth** is that which is void of error and possessing liberating power to completely support vision development and fulfillment*

3 Key elements:

- **Actuality:** reality
- **Authenticity:** genuine
- **Authority:** power

This principle reveals to us that biblical truth is a completely reliable, unadulterated, trustworthy and honest report. We have to believe that the information contained in the Bible is of the highest level of integrity. If we cannot accept this premise to be the foundation on which we base our trust, then our trust is unfounded. The principle definition tells us that we must conclude that truth is void of error while possessing the liberating power to completely support our efforts in vision development and fulfillment.

The seventh principle in the remedy for fear reveals to us perfect composure. Job 5:19-22.

Job 5:19 He shall deliver thee in six troubles: yea, in seven there shall no evil touch thee.

Job 5:20 In famine he shall redeem thee from death: and in war from the power of the sword.

Job 5:21 Thou shalt be hid from the

scourge of the tongue: neither shalt thou be afraid of destruction when it cometh.

Job 5:22   At destruction and famine thou shalt laugh: neither shalt thou be afraid of the beasts of the earth.

Job reminds us in verse 19 of the ability of God to deliver us, no matter how devastating an experience may be.   He points out that in six troubles He will deliver us, and in the seventh no evil will be able to touch us.

Occasionally, I like to study numbers as they are presented in the Bible.   The number seven usually suggest a completion.   Job said in the seventh trial, or the time where it will look like total destruction is coming, it will not touch you.

In verse 20 Job says that even in a famine we will be redeemed from death.   If war breaks out on every side, its weapons will not harm us.

In verse 21 he says we will be hidden from the scourge of tongues coming against us. Therefore, we will be protected from destruction when it comes.   The rise of this destruction cannot overwhelm us.   He concludes in verse 22 that neither destruction nor famine can steal our joy.   The beast of the earth will not strike terror in our hearts.

The eighth principle in the remedy for fear is a

bold determination. Proverbs 28:1.

Prov 28:1 ¶ The wicked flee when no man pursueth: but the righteous are bold as a lion.

David says that there are people who run when it appears that no one is chasing them. But, the righteous are as bold as a lion.

The ninth principle in the remedy for fear is security in every situation. Isaiah 43:2.

Isa 43:2 When thou passest through the waters, I *will be* with thee; and through the rivers, they shall not overflow thee: when thou walkest through the fire, thou shalt not be burned; neither shall the flame kindle upon thee.

The prophet says we may pass through waters that would attempt to drown us, but God is with us and the waters will not overflow us. There may be heated situations whose fire may consume every set of circumstances and benefits around us, but we will not be burned. No fire will ignite upon us. We are not kindling for any heated situation.

The tenth principle in the remedy for fear is

no more human harassments, depicted in Hebrews 13:6.

Heb 13:6 So that we may boldly say, The Lord is my helper, and I will not fear what man shall do unto me.

The apostle Paul wants us to understand that we can boldly say God is our helper. With that thought in mind, there is no fear in us of what any man can do unto us.

The eleventh principle in the remedy for fear is serene sleep, as depicted in Psalms 3:5 and Proverbs 3: 23-25.

Ps 3:5 I laid me down and slept; I awaked; for the LORD sustained me.

David says, "When I lay down to sleep God will awaken me because it is He who sustains me." He further says that, "I will walk in my ways safely and my foot will be as solid as a rock."

Solomon says in Proverbs 3:23-25, "I will not give up for I will lay down and my sleep will be sweet."

Prov 3:23 Then shalt thou walk in thy way safely, and thy foot shall not stumble.

Prov 3:24 When thou liest down, thou shalt not be afraid: yea, thou shalt lie down, and thy sleep shall be sweet.

Prov 3:25 Be not afraid of sudden fear, neither of the desolation of the wicked, when it cometh.

It is absolutely critical that you and I begin to understand that fear has no place in our hearts. There are many passages of Scripture that reveal to us that fear and faith cannot successfully stay in the heart of the believer. We must deny fear the chance of successfully achieving its mandate in our lives. Remember, there is no fear in love. Perfect love cast out fear.